DEVELOPMENT EFFECTIVENESS BRIEF

BHUTAN AND
THE ASIAN DEVELOPMENT BANK
PARTNERSHIP FOR INCLUSIVE GROWTH

OCTOBER 2020

ASIAN DEVELOPMENT BANK

ADB

CONTENTS

Bhutan Development Indicators   iv

Introduction   1

An Inclusive Vision of Growth: In Support of Gross National Happiness   4

    Promoting Gender Equality in a More Vibrant Labor Market   5

    Building Better Transport Networks: Deepening Regional Integration and   9
    Connecting Rural Populations

    Designing Livable Cities that Feel Like Home   12

    Resilient Growth: Hydropower to Drive the Economy   15

    Extending Access to Finance and Supporting Money Management 19

Improving Operational Effectiveness and Services   21

Moving Forward   23

Bhutan Development Indicators

Indicator	Benchmark Year	Year with Most Current Data
Population (million)	0.60 [2000][a]	0.73 [2017][a]
	634,982 [2005][b]	727,145 [2017][b]
Population growth rate (annual % change)[a]	1.30 [2000]	1.30 [2017][b]
Share of population in urban areas (% of total population)[a][c]	33.65 [2012]	37.80 [2017]
	30.9 [2005][b]	37.8 [2017][b]
GDP ($ billion, current)[a]	1.83 [FY2014]	2.64 [FY2018]
GDP per capita ($ current)[a]	2,455.2 [FY2014]	3,555.1 [FY2018]
Unemployment rate (%)[d]	2.6 [2014]	2.7 [2019]
Women[d]	3.5 [2014]	3.3 [2019]
Men[d]	1.9 [2014]	2.2 [2019]
Youth unemployment rate (%)[d]	9.4 [2014]	11.9 [2019]
Women[d]	10.0 [2014]	13.8 [2019]
Men[d]	8.6 [2014]	9.7 [2019]
Population below poverty line (%)[a]	31.70 [2003]	8.20 [2017]
Infant mortality rate (below 1 year/per 1,000 live births)[a]	59.40 [2000]	25.60 [2017]
Life expectancy at birth (years)[a]	60.29 [2000]	70.20 [2016]
Population with access to safe drinking water (%)[a]	86.10 [2000]	98.00 [2017]
Population with access to sanitation (%)[a]	38.70 [2000]	74.80 [2017]
Population with access to electricity (%)	92.0 [2012][e]	99.9 [2017][f]
Urban	99.6 [2012][e]	100 [2017][f]
Rural	87.3 [2012][e]	98.0 [2017][f]
Installed generation capacity (MWp)[g]	1,498.83 [2014]	2,342.74 [2019]

FY = fiscal year, GDP = gross domestic product, MWp = mega-watt peak.
a   Asian Development Bank (ADB). 2019. Bhutan: Country Partnership Strategy (2019–2023). Manila. August.
b   Government of Bhutan, National Statistics Bureau. 2018. 2017 Population and Housing Census of Bhutan. Thimpu.
c   ADB. 2014. Bhutan: Country Partnership Strategy (2014–2018). Manila. June.
d   Government of Bhutan, National Statistics Bureau. 2019. 2019 Labour Force Survey Report, Bhutan.
e   ADB; and Government of Bhutan, National Statistics Bureau. 2013. Bhutan Living Standards Survey 2012 Report. Manila and Thimpu.
f   Government of Bhutan, National Statistics Bureau. 2017. Bhutan Living Standards Survey Report 2017. Thimpu.
g   Government of Bhutan, National Statistics Bureau. 2019. 2019 Statistical Yearbook of Bhutan. Thimphu.

Source: Asian Development Bank.

INTRODUCTION

The Kingdom of Bhutan is nestled within the Himalayan mountain range, and shares land borders on all sides with India and the People's Republic of China. With elevations climbing from 160 meters (m) to 7,314 m above sea level, Bhutan's topography poses logistical challenges to connectivity, trade, and inclusive growth. Despite this, the country has made remarkable progress to develop its infrastructure and economy while preserving its pristine environment and vibrant culture.

Bhutan became a member of the Asian Development Bank (ADB) in 1982 and processed its first loan the following year. For nearly four decades, ADB has played a major role in supporting governance reforms in Bhutan and scaling up the nation's infrastructure. In response to Bhutan's development needs and limited financial resources, ADB has delivered most of its assistance in the form of concessional loans and grants, through its Asian Development Fund.

Protecting the environment. Bhutan has been able to strike a balance between economic development and environmental conservation. Today, the country has over 70% forest coverage (photo by Tshering Lhamo/ADB).

Today, ADB is Bhutan's largest multilateral development partner, with total commitments reaching $927.12 million in February 2020, spread across 200 projects and technical assistance (TA) initiatives. ADB's physical investments have focused on energy, transport, and water and other urban infrastructure and services. Nonphysical interventions have supported capacity building and policy dialogue to improve financial management and support good governance (figure).[1]

---

1   Bhutan saw a peaceful transition from an absolute monarchy to a constitutional democratic monarchy in 2008 and has since placed increasing focus on decentralizing its system of governance.

Cumulative Lending, Grant, and Technical Assistance Commitments for Bhutan
(as of 29 February 2020) (%)

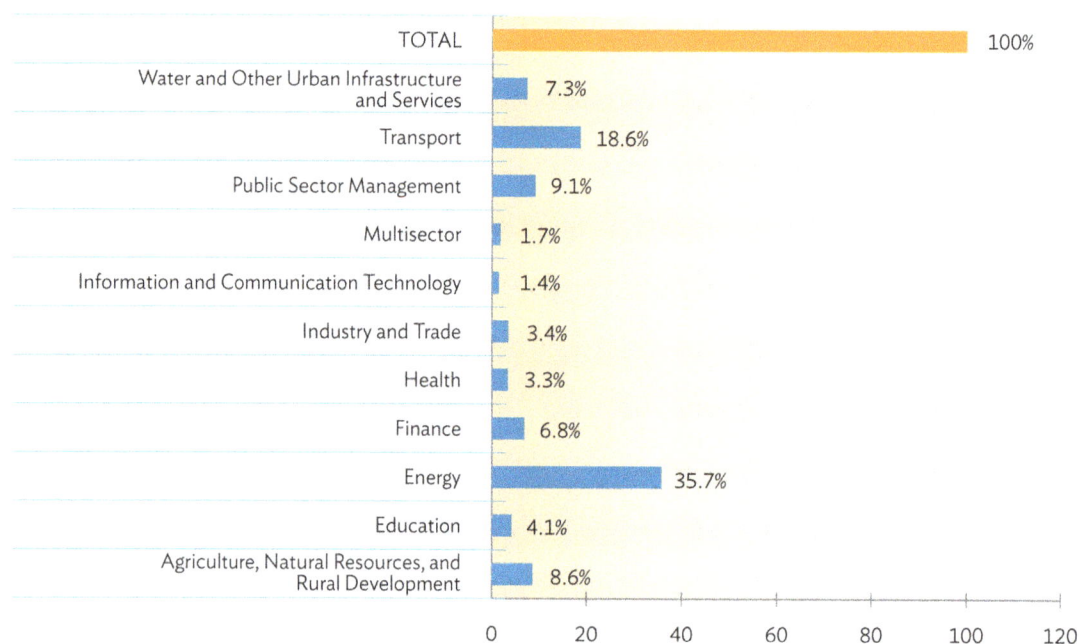

Sector	%
TOTAL	100%
Water and Other Urban Infrastructure and Services	7.3%
Transport	18.6%
Public Sector Management	9.1%
Multisector	1.7%
Information and Communication Technology	1.4%
Industry and Trade	3.4%
Health	3.3%
Finance	6.8%
Energy	35.7%
Education	4.1%
Agriculture, Natural Resources, and Rural Development	8.6%

Source: Asian Development Bank.

Loan and Grant Approvals in Bhutan
($ million)

Year	1983–2013	2014	2015	2016	2017	2018	2019	Total
OCR	51.00	70.00	0	0	0	0	0	121.00
ADF	422.85	100.85	36.20	27.87	0	98.00	30.00	715.77
TA	54.89	10.95	4.80	2.84	1.20	1.00	2.73	78.40
JFPR	11.44	0	0	0	0	0	0	11.44
Others	1.00	0	0	0	0	0	0	1.00
Total	541.18	181.80	41.00	30.71	1.20	99.00	32.73	927.61

Note: Numbers may not sum precisely because of rounding.
ADF = Asian Development Fund, OCR = ordinary capital resources, JFPR = Japan Fund for Poverty Reduction,
TA = technical assistance.
Source: Asian Development Bank.

Projects and TA have translated to significant economic and development gains, with the economy expanding at an average 7% per year from fiscal year (FY) 1998 to FY2018, and the poverty rate falling by more than half, from 23% in 2007 to 8.2% in 2017 (table). While Bhutan is currently on the United Nation's list of least developed countries, it has made tremendous progress in driving socioeconomic development, and expects to graduate from the list in 2023.

Despite progress to date, Bhutan's economic expansion has been driven narrowly by the hydropower sector and skewed toward a single trade partner. Power sales alone, primarily to India, contribute about 25% to total gross domestic product annually, account for 32% of total exports, and generate about 25% of the government's total domestic revenue. At the same time, existing transport infrastructure is not adequate to support increased trade and economic diversification, and urban environments need further investment to absorb the influx of rural populations.

More than half of Bhutan's 734,374 residents live in rural areas, and about two-thirds of the workforce is engaged in subsistence farming. However, as the nation continues to undergo rapid economic transformation, its people are migrating to cities to find work. There is an urgent need for Bhutan to diversify its economy to create more jobs and provide equal access to opportunity.

Amid rapid transformation, the government has emphasized the need to continue preserving the nation's vibrant culture and pristine environment while extending the benefits of economic growth to all.

Urban development in the capital city, Thimphu. Bhutan has witnessed unprecedented levels of socioeconomic development since opening up to modern development in the early 1960s (photo by Eric Sales/ADB).

Bhutan is changing fast. The economy is expanding, its governance structure is decentralizing, and the country is building an extensive network of transport, energy, and urban infrastructure. Amid rapid transformation, the government has emphasized the need to continue preserving the nation's vibrant culture and pristine environment while extending the benefits of economic growth to all. ADB is supporting Bhutan to distribute the benefits of its economic transformation across the population, in line with the nation's unique vision of development.

AN INCLUSIVE VISION OF GROWTH: IN SUPPORT OF GROSS NATIONAL HAPPINESS

Bhutan's development goals are rooted in the concept of gross national happiness, which seeks to balance material and nonmaterial values for holistic human thriving—or, put simply, happiness for all.[2] The government articulates its development goals through five-year plans, in line with the guiding ideals of gross national happiness.

ADB's country partnership strategies (CPS) reflect the interplay of Bhutan's five-year plans and ADB's strategic frameworks, including Strategy 2020 and Strategy 2030.[3] ADB implemented the CPS, 2014–2018 in parallel with Bhutan's Eleventh Five Year Plan, seeking to drive economic growth, expand connectivity infrastructure, and improve the quality of life in urban centers.

The objectives of the CPS, 2014–2018 mirrored the guiding principles of the Eleventh Five-Year Plan: self-reliance to meet all development needs by 2020, inclusive social development to reduce poverty and inequality, and green growth to ensure carbon-neutral development.[4] In line with requests from the government, ADB's support during 2014–2018 continued to focus on clean energy, roads and aviation transport, and urban infrastructure.

ADB has focused on these infrastructure sectors in Bhutan since the CPS, 2006–2010 but scaled up assistance in new areas—including information and communication technology, aviation, and trade. During 2014–2018, ADB leveraged its comparative advantage in these sectors to make Bhutan's growth more inclusive.

To do so, the portfolio addressed gender equality, job creation, regional integration, and financial inclusion. ADB's support during 2014–2018 helped lay the foundations for a more inclusive economy. It assisted the government to increase access to finance—which will enable people across the nation to open businesses—and helped communities develop the skills they needed to participate meaningfully in the economy. Assistance during 2014–2018 supported ADB's vision to foster a prosperous, inclusive, resilient, and sustainable Asia and the Pacific within Bhutan's unique cultural, geographic, and political ecosystem.

---

2   Center for Bhutan Studies & GNH (Gross National Happiness). https://www.grossnationalhappiness.com/.
3   ADB. 2006. *Bhutan: Country Strategy and Program*. Manila; ADB. 2008. *Strategy 2020: The Long-Term Strategic Framework of the Asian Development Bank, 2008–2020*. Manila; ADB. 2014. *Bhutan: Country Partnership Strategy (2014–2018)*. Manila; ADB. 2018. *Strategy 2030: Achieving a Prosperous, Inclusive, Resilient, and Sustainable Asia and the Pacific*. Manila.
4   Royal Government of Bhutan, Gross National Happiness Commission. 2013. Eleventh Five Year Plan, 2013–2018. Thimphu.

At a fabric shop in Thimphu. In Bhutan, women are engaged in mostly small businesses (photo by Eric Sales/ ADB).

Promoting Gender Equality in a More Vibrant Labor Market

Bhutan's economy is thriving, but the private sector is not creating enough jobs to distribute the benefits of growth. Women and youth, in particular, struggle to find work in the formal economy, and unemployment is on the rise. At the same time, youth represent a large portion of the country's demographic composition, and improvements in education are likely to increase demand for skilled jobs outside of the agriculture sector.[5] Creating equal access to jobs, and the skills to earn employment, is at the heart of ADB's work to reduce poverty and support inclusive, gender-balanced economic growth in Bhutan.

ADB is helping the public and private sectors create new employment opportunities, while supporting people across Bhutan to participate meaningfully in the economy. Crucially, ADB is focusing on gender balance in the labor market to ensure equal access to opportunity.

Two initiatives completed during 2014–2018—the Advancing Economic Opportunities for Women and Girls project and TA for Decentralized Coordination and Partnerships for Gender Equality Results—helped increase balanced participation in the workforce, while supporting the government to monitor and scale up progress on gender mainstreaming.

Creating equal access to jobs, and the skills to earn employment, is at the heart of ADB's work to reduce poverty and support inclusive, gender-balanced economic growth in Bhutan.

---

5   The median age of Bhutan's population is 26.9 years old, against the international average of 30. The youth unemployment rate is 11.9% (13.8% for females and 9.8% for males).

The Advancing Economic Opportunities for Women and Girls project introduced new ways for women to earn livelihoods while developing stronger roles in their communities. It also empowered civil society organizations (CSOs) to further drive gender-balanced economic growth.

In addition to providing hands-on learning opportunities at the community level, the project addressed gender equality from the top-down. It introduced an automated gender monitoring system for government agencies to assess gender dynamics in the public and private sectors, and built capacity to implement gender action plans.

The project's key results include the following:

82 gender focal points
from the government (32 female and 50 male) trained to develop and monitor gender mainstreaming strategies

67% of government agencies
developed and approved sector-specific gender strategies

386 rural villagers
(254 women and 132 men) received skills training in repairing household appliances, tailoring, hairdressing, and embroidery

829 youth
(543 females and 286 males) paired with apprenticeship programs, with 702 (474 females and 228 males) employed at the project's completion

Training activities in rural areas were particularly impactful, as they created opportunities for women to earn an income, often for the first time. To foster sustainable growth in women-run small and medium enterprises, the grant helped convene self-help groups and establish partnerships with local nongovernment organizations.

The complementary TA for Decentralized Coordination and Partnerships for Gender Equality Results identified and addressed barriers to women's participation in the workforce. It trained representatives from all 20 of Bhutan's districts to address gender issues in the workplace, and produced three studies that were transformed into a four-part series and aired on national television.

Since the TA identified lack of affordable childcare as a major hurdle to the participation of Bhutanese women in the workforce, it established childcare centers, helped train caregivers, and set up service agreements to ensure the centers could be sustained through public–private partnerships.

In addition to reducing barriers to women's participation in the workforce, the TA created new livelihood opportunities. Working in close partnership with the government's National Commission for Women and Children and local CSOs, the TA trained self-help groups to support micro-enterprises in accessing new markets.

When asked about her experience, self-help group member Dawa Pema, in Bhutan's Zhemgang District, explained, "Our self-help group is now even able to save money on its own, which is readily available for any member when needed." Reflecting on the initiative, Tshechu—a participant in Samtse District—highlighted, "The extra income helped us meet our food and clothes expenses besides enabling us to send out children to schools, since we can now afford their education expenses too."

The TA met or exceeded all its targets:

13 childcare centers
established and 53 caregivers (49 women and 4 men) trained

18 self-help groups trained
in business development and market access (against a target of 10)

31 sustainable business agreements
signed (against a target of 20), representing ongoing commercial opportunities

386 government staff
(116 women and 270 men) trained to use the web-based gender monitoring system

57 agencies
(50 government, 4 CSOs, 1 religious, and 2 educational) began capturing real-time gender data using the gender monitoring system at the end of the TA

"The extra income helped us mete out food and clothes expenses besides enabling us to send out children to schools, since we can now afford their education expenses too."

Farming as source of food and livelihood. A woman harvests crops from her farm in Bhutan, where rice is the main staple food (photo by Eric Sales/ADB).

Both the project and the TA helped build close partnerships among government stakeholders, CSOs, and the private sector to support a more robust and gender-balanced labor market.

The key to generating more employment opportunities will be to diversify and expand the private sector, while increasing access to targeted skills training.

However, despite success in strengthening gender monitoring and creating new opportunities for women to earn an income, unemployment in Bhutan remains a persistent challenge. The youth unemployment rate actually increased from 9.4% in 2014 to 11.9% in 2019. The key to generating more employment opportunities will be to diversify and expand the private sector, while increasing access to targeted skills training.[6]

From 2014 to 2018, ADB helped Bhutan reimagine its technical and vocational education and training (TVET). TA for Institutional Strengthening for Skills Development supported the Ministry of Labor and Human Resources to create a blueprint to guide TVET development during 2016–2026. The TA led to the approval of the associated Skills Training and Education Pathways Upgrading Project in 2018, which will enable ADB to scale up much-needed support for Bhutan's TVET sector.

---

6   Developing Bhutan's finance sector—and, in turn, access to capital for businesses—is essential to create new jobs. ADB's support for the finance sector is discussed separately on pp. 19–20.

Building Better Transport Networks: Deepening Regional Integration and Connecting Rural Populations

Connectivity will also play an important role in helping Bhutan achieve more inclusive growth. Domestically, safe roads and airports are the key to unlock access to goods and opportunities, particularly for rural populations. At the regional level, efficient transport is essential to strengthen trade ties among Bhutan, India, and the broader South Asian subregion.

In line with Strategy 2030 and Bhutan's Eleventh Five-Year Plan, ADB's support to Bhutan's transport sector is fostering greater regional cooperation and integration (RCI), and advancing rural development and food security. Given Bhutan's status as a landlocked and small country, deeper RCI plays an essential role in economic diversification and accelerated private sector growth.

The transport sector accounts for 20.2% of ADB's total financing in Bhutan, making it the second largest sector of assistance after the energy sector, with 37.2%. As of December 2019, ADB had implemented a total of 30 transport projects and TAs, with cumulative financing reaching $178.42 million.

Transport operations completed during 2014–2018 delivered transformative results:

199.8 km of roads constructed
or upgraded

3 airports upgraded
to improve safety and security

1 dry port built
to improve trade efficiency

Transport Map

ADB's support to Bhutan's aviation subsector is helping bridge the rural–urban divide. It is also increasing the safety, security, and climate resilience of infrastructure. As the tourism industry continues to grow, domestic airports will help extend economic benefits to remote areas.

The Air Transport Connectivity Enhancement Project upgraded three domestic airports—Bumthang, Gelephu, and Yongphula—with essential infrastructure, including through runway pavement, security fencing, runway drainage, and flood protection. It also built a new terminal building at

Gelephu Airport. A new terminal building at Bumthang is due for completion in 2020. Upgrades scaled up airport capacity, increased access to parts of the country where road transport is limited, and helped improve air transport connectivity in Bhutan.

Dasho Tashi Wangmo, Member of Parliament, frequently uses the flight services to Yongphula to visit her family. She said that operationalization of Yongphula Airport had greatly benefited people in at least five eastern districts, and was worth the investment. Gewog Head Gup Kinzang also acknowledged the benefits of Yongphula Airport, underlining its importance in opening the east of the kingdom to its west and making travel easier, safer, and faster.[7] Bishnu Maya Gurung, who sends her son to Sherubtse College by plane, said that air travel was safer, faster, and less troublesome for her son.

Not only have travel times reduced by days but also there is now no longer any risk of being stranded on the road as a results of monsoon landslides and winter snow blockades on the mountain passes.

—Dasho Tashi Wangmo, Member of Parliament

Winding road in the mountains. Bhutan and ADB continue to invest heavily in critical economic infrastructure to enhance the economic prospects and well-being of people (photo by Eric Sales/ADB).

The project helped increase the total number of passengers carried on the national airline, Druk Air, and Tashi Air from 299,429 in 2014 to 398,391 in 2018.

—Bishnu Maya Gurung, Bhutanese national

As a landlocked and mountainous country, Bhutan relies heavily on its road network. However, with 62% of the population dispersed across rural and remote areas, people often need to walk several hours to reach a road—limiting their ability to access markets and essential resources like schools, health outposts, and financial institutions. ADB's support to the construction of farm roads has

7 A *gewog* is a county under a district in Bhutan.

significantly improved access to roads. In 2012, 42.2% of Bhutan's total population had to travel two hours or more to reach a farm road; this number had dropped to 16.6% in 2017.[8]

The Farm Roads to Support Poor Farmers' Livelihoods project, financed by the Japan Fund for Poverty Reduction, has built 25 km of roads in Chhukha and Trashigang districts and increased access to economic opportunities and social services for 470 households. New roads in Trashigang district, for example, have reduced the portion of the population living more than an hour's walk from a road from 85% to 24%.

Sellers and their produce by the roadside. Farm roads provide easy market access and empower women to participate in trade and contribute to income generation (photo by Eric Sales/ADB).

The project also provided training to farmers on how to access finance and technical resources to increase agricultural productivity. The new roads and training have helped farmers sell more produce and decrease poverty in the project areas from 30% to 16% of the population.

Yeshey Nidup, a bank employee from Bongo village, has witnessed the socioeconomic transformation the farm road has enabled. He said, "People in the village have started commercial farming on a large scale. Cultivation of high-value cardamom and oranges has increased people's income level, which has resulted in improvement in living conditions." He also explained, "A noticeable benefit I feel proud to mention is that the road connection has curbed rural–urban migration. Many retired office goers have settled down in the village. After the road [was completed], I also see many new houses built with proper sanitation like attached toilets. The village now looks prosperous."

In addition to supporting domestic access to opportunity, Bhutan is scaling up its road network and harmonizing customs procedure to streamline regional trade. Commerce with India accounts for 76% of Bhutan's exports (including power), and over 85% of its imports. Improving road connectivity and customs administration with India is essential to strengthen trade efficiency with Bhutan's immediate neighbor, but also to scale up the movement of goods across the region.

New roads and training have helped farmers sell more produce and decrease poverty in the project areas from 30% to 16% of the population.

---

8 Government of Bhutan, National Statistics Bureau. 2012. Bhutan Living Standards Survey, 2012 Report. Thimphu; Government of Bhutan, National Statistics Bureau. 2017. Bhutan Living Standards Survey, 2017 Report. Thimphu.

The South Asia Subregional Economic Cooperation (SASEC) program is a flagship initiative, designed to strengthen cross-border connectivity, trade, and economic cooperation between seven South Asian nations, including Bhutan.[9] Since 2001, it has mobilized more than $12.5 billion in support of RCI.

In 2012, ADB launched the SASEC Trade Facilitation program to streamline the movement of people and goods across borders, in and out of Bangladesh, Bhutan, and Nepal. The program helped modernize customs procedures with the aim of developing more efficient, transparent, secure, and service-oriented trade processes. It also contributed to policy changes, trade infrastructure, and capacity building for 1,800 officials (of whom 820 were women), and will support more robust RCI across the SASEC subregion.

Designing Livable Cities that Feel Like Home

People across Bhutan are moving to cities. The share of the population living in urban areas grew from 30.9% in 2005 to 37.8% in 2017; by 2050, about half of the population will live in urban centers.

Without proper planning, Bhutan's rapid urban migration threatens essential services, including water, sanitation, and hygiene, at the same time increasing traffic congestion. Effective city planning can improve the quality of life for thousands, while dramatically enhancing resource efficiency and urban resilience to the effects of climate change. Support to clean water, sanitation, and hygiene has direct impacts on public health, by ensuring waste is managed effectively and that communities follow best practices for hygiene and safety. As Bhutan's population continues to move to urban centers, well-designed, livable cities can become a vector of inclusion—they can help distribute resources more evenly and increase access to opportunity.

Effective city planning can improve the quality of life for thousands, while dramatically enhancing resource efficiency and urban resilience to the effects of climate change.

Designing livable cities. The sun shines brightly on the Buddha Dordenma statue overlooking Thimphu City (photo by Eric Sales/ADB).

9   The seven participating countries are Bangladesh, Bhutan, India, Maldives, Myanmar, Nepal, and Sri Lanka.

ADB is helping Bhutan plan, construct, and manage vibrant urban centers. Support to the urban, water, and sanitation sectors in Bhutan is carefully aligned with Strategy 2030's focus on building livable cities, and the national objective to "improve livability, safety and sustainability of human settlements through access to adequate affordable housing, efficient and effective municipal services, and clean and green public spaces for social engagement.[10]" Over the course of its partnership with Bhutan, ADB has mobilized a cumulative $63.0 million in grants and loans to support urban, water, and sanitation initiatives, representing about 7.5% of its total assistance to the country.

From 2006 to 2016, ADB implemented the Urban Infrastructure Development Project, which helped transform the way of life in three urban areas— Dagana, Phuentsholing, and Thimphu. The project delivered physical investments to improve transport, drainage, water supply, and sanitation. It also supported increased hygiene and sanitation through awareness raising campaigns, and by making physical investments in drainage, wastewater collection, and treatment facilities. To ensure the sustainability of results, it also targeted efficient operation and maintenance of key infrastructure, and helped raise community awareness of proper solid waste management practices. Improvements to roadside drainage reduced flooding in Thimphu, and in turn helped improve urban resilience to the effects of climate change.

Crucially, the project piloted a new land-pooling approach to urban development, which made city improvements and project results possible in the nation's capital city, Thimphu. The land-pooling approach encouraged landowners to share plots of their land on which to develop public urban goods—including parks, playgrounds, and sporting facilities—to support a more vibrant urban community.

> **Land-pooling encouraged land owners to share plots of their land on which to develop public urban goods—including parks, playgrounds, and sporting facilities—to support a more vibrant urban community in the capital.**

96,840 people
benefited from the project

63,360 people
benefited from new roads

64,642 people
received a new supply of safe water

37.2 km of improved road and drainage
were constructed:
33.7 km in Thimphu
2.4 km in Phuentsholing
1.1 km in Dagana

---

10 Royal Government of Bhutan, Gross National Happiness Commission. 2019. Twelfth Five-Year Plan, 2018–2023. Thimphu. Note that ADB's support to the urban and water sectors in Bhutan is also closely aligned with National Key Results Areas (NKRAs) in the Eleventh Five-Year Plan (including NKRA 5: water security and NKRA 11: improved public service delivery); as well as with those outlined in the Twelfth Five-Year Plan (including NKRA 15: sustainable human settlements, NKRA 17: sustainable water, and NKRA 9: infrastructure, communication, and public services).

2 new water treatment plants
and 27 km of supply networks were constructed:
6,500 m³/day in Thimphu
300 m³/day in Dagana

12,800 household connections
to wastewater treatment were made possible, with associated treatment and safe disposal facilities (drying beds or septic tanks)
28.5 km of wastewater collection networks

Whatever development happened would not have happened without land pooling. Nothing would have taken off. So many buildings were constructed, all because land pooling was successful. It allowed us to get areas where roads could be built. [Without it] this wasn't the case. Acquisition of land to build roads would have taken ages. And land pooling is a very fair scheme—everybody contributes for the land development. Other countries can look to this as a successful model.

— Kinlay Dorjee, Mayor of Thimphu.

Discussing projects and initiatives.
Thimphu Mayor Kinlay Dorjee during an interview session (photo by Kinlay Dorjee/ADB).

Resilient Growth: Hydropower to Drive the Economy

Bhutan isn't just carbon neutral; it is carbon negative. Home to some of the most biodiverse ecosystems on the planet, Bhutan enjoys 71% forest cover and is the only country in the world to absorb more carbon than it emits.[11] It also exports carbon-neutral electricity to India—helping its neighbor to the south reduce emissions as well.

ADB has played a key role in developing Bhutan's hydropower industry. Strategy 2030 emphasizes tackling climate change, building climate and disaster resilience, and enhancing environmental sustainability, while Bhutan's Eleventh Five-Year Plan highlights the importance of green growth, through power generation and preserving its forests.[12]

Bhutan's vision of sustainable growth recognizes the value of protecting its water resources for generations to come. ADB has played a key role in supporting Bhutan to plan and implement measures to increase resilience to climate change through water resource management.

Hydropower as an economic mainstay in Bhutan. A tower being installed for the Dagachhu Hydropower Plant as part of the Green Power Development Project (photo by Eric Sales/ADB).

In 2019, the country's total installed power generation capacity was 2,342 mega-watt peak (MWp).[13] With the exception of a few hundred solar panels, some wind turbines, and a handful of small diesel generators, all power in Bhutan is produced sustainably—by water.

---

11 Royal Government of Bhutan, National Environment Commission. 2015. Communication of Intended Nationally Determined Contribution. Thimphu. In 2000, Bhutan's forests sequestered approximately 6.3 million tons of carbon dioxide equivalent, while annual emissions in the same year were about 1.6 million tons.

12 Bhutan has pledged to keep 60% of its land covered in forests as a part of its Constitution and commitment to carbon neutrality.

13 This includes 720 MWp from the Mangdechhu hydropower plant, commissioned in August 2019.

In addition to
constructing
the third largest
power plant in
the country,
the Green
Power Project
has supported
Bhutan to
achieve a 99.9%
electrification
rate across the
country.

ADB's support has helped construct nearly one-tenth of all installed power generation capacity in Bhutan. The Green Power Development Project built the Dagachhu hydroelectric plant, which has an installed capacity of 126 MWp, and supplies about 515 gigawatt-hour (GWh) of power to India each year. During 2015–2019, the Dagachhu plant alone generated an average of $16.5 million per year in power export sales to India.

In addition to constructing the third largest power plant in the country, the Green Power Project has supported Bhutan to achieve a 99.9% electrification rate across the country. The project included a grant that connected thousands of new households to the electricity grid, and installed solar panels in areas where grid connections were not feasible.

Overall, the project delivered the following results:

126 MW of hydropower generation installed
515 GWh produced by Dagachhu and exported to India in 2015

$16.5 million
for the Bhutanese economy each year

19 km of transmission lines constructed
9,586 households
connected to electricity grids

163 solar power systems installed
116 remote schools, health stations, and monasteries
receiving off-grid solar power

Sustainable energy sources. Bhutan is diversifying energy sources to harness the potential of solar and wind power, which provides livelihood opportunities for low-income households (photo by Nidup Tshering/ADB).

The project set new trends in Bhutan and globally. It was the first public–private partnership in the Bhutanese power sector, and the first cross-border project in the world to earn Certified Emission Reductions under the United Nations' Clean Development Mechanism.[14] The project is not only contributing to Bhutan's economic growth and reducing emissions but also delivering a variety of co-benefits to local populations. These co-benefits include access to stable and low-cost power, local employment generation, and health benefits associated with reduction in air pollution by shifting from firewood to electrical appliances for cooking and heating.

Building on the project's success, ADB and the government launched the Second Green Power Development project (Nikachhu Hydropower Project) in 2015 and began construction in 2016. Phase II will install an additional 118 MWp of hydropower, in support of continued green economic growth.

Bhutan's vision of sustainable growth recognizes the value of protecting its water resources for generations to come. At the same time, the nation is cognizant of the severe threats that climate change poses, and in particular the impacts it can have on water security across the agriculture, energy, and urban sectors.

Integrated water resource management is, therefore, essential to safeguard Bhutan's people, economy, and future, in the face of climate change.

Bhutan's vision of sustainable growth recognizes the value of protecting its water resources for generations to come.

---

14 Certified Emission Reductions are a saleable carbon accounting instrument. They enable projects that generate carbon reductions to monetize positive environmental benefits. These are the main accounting instruments under the Kyoto Protocol to the United Nations Framework Convention on Climate Change.

ADB has played a key role in supporting Bhutan to plan and implement measures to increase resilience to climate change through water resource management. An ADB TA for Adapting to Climate Change through Integrated Water Resources Management supported the government to identify and account for key water resources and to operationalize plans to care for them well into the future.

Hydropower capabilities.
In Bhutan, hydroelectricity is generated mainly through run-of-the-river schemes (photo by Eric Sales/ADB).

The TA helped operationalize Bhutan's 2011 Water Act and related regulations, finalize the National Integrated Water Resources Management Plan, and disseminate knowledge on resilience and Bhutan's extensive water networks through a colorful publication titled *Water: Securing Bhutan's Future*.[15] The TA also helped develop a river basin master plan, an irrigation master plan, and Bhutan's Water Security Index—which provides a framework for planning, monitoring, and interagency collaboration—to protect Bhutan's water resources.

15 ADB and Government of Bhutan, National Environment Commission. 2016. *Water: Securing Bhutan's Future.* Government of Bhutan, National Environment Commission. 2016. National Integrated Water Resources Management Plan. Thimphu.

Extending Access to Finance and Supporting Money Management

Broadening its economic base is the key for Bhutan to increase job opportunities, build economic resilience, and enter a sustainable growth trajectory. In particular, Bhutan needs to establish a robust finance sector that can provide capital for small and medium enterprises to diversify the private sector. ADB's support has helped lay the foundations for an inclusive economy, continued partnership with the public and private sectors will help bring this to life.

From 2014 to 2018, ADB completed projects and TA totaling more than $77 million to support economic reforms, good governance, and a more dynamic financial sector. The assistance helped Bhutan regain macroeconomic stability, following a major liquidity crisis in 2012, while beginning to expand financial inclusion.[16]

ADB's support to good governance and economic reforms aligned closely with the government's objective of "self-reliance and inclusive green socioeconomic development" outlined in its Eleventh Five-Year Plan (footnote 3). The assistance package was also carefully aligned with Strategy 2030's focus on strengthening governance and institutional capacity to create an enabling environment for sustainable growth.

As a part of its public financial management support, ADB assisted Bhutan to develop a revenue administration management information system, which has helped the Department of Revenue and Customs streamline tax collection and reduce associated costs. Personal income tax (PIT), business income tax, and corporate income tax can now be paid online. Wangdi Drugyel, Commissioner, Tax Administration Division, Department of Revenue and Customs, said, "The system is helpful, and about 70% of PIT is now paid online. We are conducting awareness workshops to inform people about using the online system." Associated reforms have improved governance and public financial management, and are continuing to produce profound impacts on people's lives.

The Strengthening Economic Management Program provided $72.5 million, spread across two phases. The first phase provided policy support in four core areas, to improve (i) budget and debt management, (ii) revenue and tax collection, (iii) capital and financial markets, and (iv) internal and external audit functions. It leveraged five supporting TA initiatives to successfully stabilize the economy, ease inflation, and address the rupee shortage.[17]

However, sustainable improvements to governance and macroeconomic management take time. Recognizing this, ADB is providing ongoing, systematic support to strengthen Bhutan's economy and diversify its private sector. The second phase of the Strengthening Economic Management Program built on successful reforms initiated during the first phase but increased the focus on strengthening Bhutan's financial markets.

ADB is providing ongoing, systematic support to strengthen Bhutan's economy and diversify its private sector.

---

16 India is Bhutan's largest trade partner, accounting for 75% of Bhutan's imports and 90% of its exports in 2013. Since trade is conducted in Indian rupees, it is essential for Bhutan to maintain reserves in Indian currency. However, in 2012, a buildup of public spending, paired with poor liquidity management, led to a severe shortage of rupees in Bhutan's reserves. This "rupee crunch" threatened to generate a sudden slowdown in the economy.

17 ADB. 2010. Technical Assistance to Bhutan for Strengthening Public Management in Bhutan. Manila; ADB. 2011. Technical Assistance to Bhutan for Developing a Revenue Administration Management Information System. Manila; ADB. 2012. Technical Assistance to Bhutan for Capital Market Development. Manila; ADB. 2012. Technical Assistance for Supporting Financial Stability in Bhutan and Maldives. Manila.

In addition to providing continued support to macroeconomic management, the second phase developed financial literacy programs and helped support deeper financial inclusion. The program delivered trainings targeting different socioeconomic, demographic, gender, and age groups. It also supported Bhutan Development Bank to expand its branchless banking service—enabling more than 10,000 people to open bank accounts, with women accounting for more than half of the new accounts.

Knowledge sharing and skills development. Government officials attend training on portfolio administration and gender mainstreaming in Thimphu (photo by ADB).

IMPROVING OPERATIONAL EFFECTIVENESS AND SERVICES

Enhanced field presence. ADB's Bhutan Resident Mission helps provide customized solutions according to the country's needs (photo by Kinley Tshering/ADB).

In 2014, ADB established a resident mission in Thimphu, reflecting its commitment to scale up partnerships with the government and its development partners and to continue deepening the impacts of its investments in Bhutan. ADB's staff resources in Bhutan have increased from two staff members in 2014 to nine during 2017–2020.

Reflecting lessons learned while implementing the Country Partnership Strategy (CPS), 2014–2018, ADB's resident mission will play a pivotal role in strengthening two core operational areas going forward—program efficiency and sustainability.

The performance of ADB's assistance program in Bhutan during 2014–2018 was successful overall, though performance measures decreased slightly compared with the previous CPS period. ADB's support during 2014–2018 remained relevant and effective, with projects closely aligned with country needs and priorities, and with most initiatives meeting or exceeding targets.

However, ADB's efficiency implementing projects during 2014–2018 was a concern. Delays in project implementation, cost increases, and misalignments of project activities—notably safeguard operations—weighed down process efficiency, although they did not jeopardize the overall viability of projects.

Bhutan's rugged, mountainous terrain makes it difficult to build and maintain infrastructure. During 2014–2018, limited assessments of land conditions negatively affected project efficiency. Bhutan's challenging topography, in turn, highlights the need for detailed geotechnical analysis in the early design phases of project preparation in the future.

For example, the Farm Roads to Support Poor Farmers' Livelihoods project estimated the cost per km of road at $61,000. This figure increased significantly to $77,178 during implementation, as a result of the unforeseen need to build a bridge and to make other costly physical adjustments. Similarly, a discrepancy in the detailed design led to delays and cost overruns during implementation of the Air Transport Connectivity Enhancement Project. Recognizing Bhutan's complex topography and the importance of reducing risks during the design stage and the potential effects on implementation efficiency, ADB will work with the executing agency to improve detailed design during project preparation.

With respect to project sustainability, ADB's Independent Evaluation Department has identified two areas for improvement: projects should secure sources of funding for operation and maintenance early on and provide ongoing capacity building for government counterparts.

Although infrastructure projects in the transport and urban sectors have delivered high-quality assets, the Farm Roads to Support Poor Farmers' Livelihoods project and the Road Network Project II appear to lack sustainable sources of funding to ensure long-term operation and maintenance. Similarly, although the Urban Infrastructure Development Project has established an extensive network of water and waste management assets, the tariff structure for solid waste management in Dagana is insufficient to cover operation and maintenance. ADB has responded by scaling up capacity building support—providing training to thousands of local government officials on diverse topics ranging from procurement and financial management to project design, risk management, and safeguards.

In response to the lessons learned during 2014–2018, ADB will implement several measures to strengthen efficiency and support long-term project sustainability. Going forward, ADB will provide additional support to ensure a higher degree of project readiness, prior to implementation. This will reduce the risks of starting a project with design flaws and help avoid corresponding delays. ADB's support to readiness will also involve establishing a project implementation office and recruiting staff early on, commencing land acquisition and resettlement processes, and completing advanced procurement actions prior to implementation. ADB has started providing complementary TA to improve the efficiency of project administration in Bhutan, including financial management and procurement. To further ensure sustainability of projects after completion, ADB will continue to build on the support provided in developing and instituting a road asset management system, by requiring better planning and additional budget allocation for operations and maintenance in projects under design. ADB will also target deeper engagement with local governments going forward.

Unlike under previous 5-year plans, resources to the local government in Bhutan's Twelfth Five-Year Plan has doubled, with an equal share of capital resources to local and central agencies. This change will encourage local governments to plan and implement capital investment projects independently. The devolution of both financial and managerial authority from the central government creates opportunities for ADB to work more closely with local governments, support capacity building, and address long-term sustainability issues.

MOVING FORWARD

ADB and Bhutan will celebrate 40 years of partnership in 2022, while implementing the CPS, 2019–2023; and in 2023 Bhutan expects to graduate from the United Nation's list of least developed countries.

Looking back over nearly four decades of partnership, ADB is proud to have supported Bhutan in achieving robust economic growth, good governance through policy dialogue and reforms, and significant infrastructure development across the energy, transport, water, and urban sectors. ADB's ongoing support will help Bhutan extend the benefits of economic growth to all of its people and establish a sustainable forward growth trajectory.

ADB and Bhutan will celebrate 40 years of partnership in 2022, while implementing the CPS, 2019–2023; and in 2023 Bhutan expects to graduate from the United Nation's list of least developed countries.

Education for all. Bhutan has achieved gender parity in primary and secondary education, and implements policies to bridge the gap in tertiary eduction (photo by Eric Sales/ADB).

The key to supporting inclusive and sustainable socioeconomic growth in Bhutan is to ensure that its people have access to the resources and opportunities they need to thrive. Over the next 5 years, ADB will help foster economic diversification and reduce disparities as its cumulative portfolio in Bhutan surpasses the $1 billion mark. ADB will also support increased resilience to climate change by providing targeted support in disaster risk reduction and associated areas.

The CPS, 2019–2023 is carefully aligned with Bhutan's Twelfth Five-Year Plan and ADB's Strategy 2030. Its three strategic pillars are (i) dynamic economic growth to foster a resilient and diversified economy, (ii) improved connectivity to provide access to information and markets, and (iii) inclusiveness through more equitable socioeconomic development.

Looking ahead, ADB will continue to invest in transport infrastructure that brings people together with opportunities, clean energy infrastructure to drive the economy, and urban and water systems to improve living standards for an increasingly urban population. In addition, ADB will support good governance and further economic reforms, in line with the vision in Bhutan's Twelfth Five-Year Plan of a "Just, Harmonious, and Sustainable Society through Enhanced Decentralization."

Given the likelihood of an economic downturn associated with the coronavirus pandemic, ADB will continue supporting Bhutan to strengthen public sector and macroeconomic management and human capital development. Interventions in public sector management and health sector development will be important to manage the current pandemic, and to enhance resilience against similar health hazards in the future and to restore macroeconomic stability and vulnerability against economic shocks. Skills development interventions will help expedite recovery in the tourism sector and address the youth unemployment problem.

Wild flowers in bloom. Bhutan is committed to ensuring environmental protection and conservation while striving to improve living standards for the population (photo by Tshering Yangzom/DGPC).

www.ingramcontent.com/pod-product-compliance
Lightning Source LLC
Chambersburg PA
CBHW040147200326

41519CB00035B/7622